A Great Idea

LEGO® Toys

by Kris Hirschmann

NORWOOD HOUSE PRESS

Norwood House Press
P.O. Box 316598
Chicago, Illinois 60631

For information regarding Norwood House Press, please visit our website at:

www.norwoodhousepress.com or call 866-565-2900.

LIBRARY OF CONGRESS CATALOGING-IN-PUBLICATION DATA

Hirschmann, Kris, 1967–
   LEGO toys / by Kris Hirschmann.
      p. cm. — (A great idea)
   Summary: "Describes the invention and development of LEGO toys. Includes glossary, websites, and bibliography for further reading"—Provided by publisher.
   Includes bibliographical references and index.
   ISBN-13: 978-1-59953-194-6 (library edition : alk. paper)
   ISBN-10: 1-59953-194-1 (library edition : alk. paper)
   1. LEGO toys—Juvenile literature. I. Title.
   TS2301.T7H562 2008
   688.7'25—dc22

                                        2008010712

Manufactured in the United States in North Mankato, Minnesota-- 164N-072010

Contents

Note: Words that are **bolded** in the text are defined in the glossary on page 44.

Chapter 1

"Only the Best"

L ife was hard in many countries in Europe in the early 1930s. Money was tight. Jobs were hard to find. This was the case in Denmark, where Ole Kirk Christiansen worked as a **master carpenter.** He struggled to make enough money to feed his family. Despite hard times, Christiansen knew that children would always need playthings. So, he decided to build wooden toys as a side business. He opened a shop in the small town of Billund in 1932. He stocked his shelves with blocks, piggy banks, and other beautifully crafted items. He hoped his toys would bring in some much-needed extra money.

Christiansen succeeded beyond his wildest dreams. The carpenter's toys were an instant hit. Business grew as news of Christiansen's work spread to nearby towns. By 1934, Christiansen had hired six employees. His toy business was doing so well that he decided to give up carpen-

Ole Kirk Christiansen created hand-made toys like these before he invented LEGO toys.

try. Christiansen called his growing business "LEGO." The name came from the Danish words *leg* and *godt*, which mean "play well." This name summed up Christiansen's hopes and dreams for his young company.

Second to None

Around the same time, Christiansen also adopted a **motto**. The motto was *Det bedste er ikke for godt*, which is Danish for "Only the best is good enough." These words reflected Ole Christiansen's feelings about quality. He used only the best materials and the most talented craftspeople. In construction, his toys were second to none.

There is a story that shows how strongly Christiansen felt about this idea. Christiansen had asked his workers to use three coats of paint on the toy wooden ducks for extra **durability**. But one worker gave the ducks only two coats of paint. The finished ducks were boxed. They were taken to the local train station for shipping. Before they could be picked up, however, Christiansen learned what his employee had done. Furious, he sent the boy to the train station to fetch the ducks. The unlucky employee spent the night in the factory, repainting the toys to meet Christiansen's high standards.

This attention to detail got results. LEGO toys were soon known across Denmark for

Brightly painted wooden toys have been popular for a very long time.

their high quality. Stores stocked them and people bought them. Christiansen hired more workers to fill the orders that piled up on his desk.

Despite his success, Christiansen was not satisfied. He came up with new **designs** for his toys. He also looked for better ways to build them. When he came across something he liked, he made it part of his business.

Plastic Arrives

In the mid-1940s, Christiansen came across a material that he thought might work well with his toys. That material was **plastic**. Plastic had been developed years earlier. It had been used for jewelry, car parts, and some other things. Few people had thought of making toys out of plastic. It had been tried at least once, though. Hilary Harry Fisher Page of England started making and selling plastic toys in 1937. He once said he liked the idea of plastic toys because of

"their **hygienic** qualities, attractive colors and absence of dangers from sharp edges and corners."

Christiansen also liked the idea of plastic toys. New processes for making and using plastic had been developed by the 1940s. Using a process called injection molding, raw plastic could be shaped into just about anything. Christiansen thought plastic would work well with his toys.

Christiansen talked to some injection molding companies about his idea. In response, a London business sent Christiansen a bag of hollow plastic bricks. The brightly colored bricks could be pushed together and taken apart for hours of building fun. The toy was **patented** in England, but not elsewhere. This meant that by law, anyone outside of England could copy and sell the bricks. The injection molding company thought LEGO could easily make something similar.

Christiansen agreed. He bought LEGO's first injection molding machine in 1947. The company's designers got to work creating new toys. Soon cars, baby rattles, and other plastic items were rolling off the LEGO production line.

The company did not, however, make the plastic bricks that Christiansen had liked so much. Although Christiansen liked the new plastic, he was a **cautious** man. He knew that people were used to wooden blocks. He did not think they would buy plastic ones. So, instead, Christiansen came up with a line of **interlocking** wooden bricks. Christiansen sent the toys out to stores, then waited to see what would happen.

An Idea Is Born

The wooden bricks were an instant success. Children loved the way they stacked together and came apart again. They were much more fun than solid blocks, which tumbled over at the slightest touch. Before long, LEGO bricks were among the company's best-selling items.

Injection Molding

Plastic toys start out as brightly colored plastic grains. The grains are stored in huge bins. They travel through tubes to an injection molding machine, which uses temperatures of up to 450 degrees Fahrenheit (232°C) to melt the grains. It injects or pushes the melted plastic into carefully shaped molds. Pressure is then applied to force the plastic into every nook and cranny of the mold. A few seconds later, the plastic is cool enough to hold its new shape. The mold opens and the new toy (or toy part) tumbles out.

A toy car that has been made of molded plastic.

Still, Christiansen was not happy. The wooden bricks had **flaws**. And this bothered him. In particular, they did not lock together as well as Christiansen would have liked. In his eyes, they were not "the best." Christiansen kept thinking about the English samples he had seen. Plastic bricks like those would surely be better than wooden ones. But would they sell? Christiansen decided to find out. He asked his designers to come up with plastic interlocking bricks. At that moment, the idea for the modern LEGO brick was born.

Kiddicraft Self-Locking Bricks

The English product that inspired Ole Kirk Christiansen was called Kiddicraft Self-Locking Bricks. The bricks were designed and patented by a **child psychologist** named Hilary Harry Fisher Page. Although LEGO would later prove that interlocking plastic bricks were a great idea, Page never made much money from his world-changing invention.

A New Way to Play

Development of the plastic bricks started in 1949. By this time Christiansen's son, Godtfred, was working side by side with his father. He helped produce the company's first line of plastic bricks.

Godtfred knew that this job meant more than just designing a new toy. LEGO bricks were going to give children a whole new way to play. Like wooden blocks, they would help kids to develop building skills. But because they stuck together, they would not fall apart by accident. This meant that kids could get creative in ways that were not possible with regular blocks. Even better, structures made with LEGO bricks were not permanent. Kids could pull the bricks apart and start all over again whenever they felt like it. Ole Kirk Christiansen felt sure that interlocking plastic bricks would be a big hit. And he was right. Chris-

Did You Know?

One of the first known games is a Babylonian board game that dates to 4000 B.C. This game is similar to the modern-day games of chess and checkers.

tiansen's simple idea would eventually change the world of toys. However, it would take years of hard work to bring this vision to life.

Chapter 2

A Simple Idea Comes to Life

The Christiansens called their new plastic toys Automatic Binding Bricks. The bricks were hollow, with open bottoms. Each brick's top bore round studs that could slide into the open bottom of another brick. Slits in the bricks' sides made them flexible enough to bend open a little bit, then snap closed to hold another brick in

Plastic LEGO bricks snap together tightly and come in many colors.

place. The bricks came in several sizes and five bright colors: red, green, yellow, blue, and white.

Problems to Overcome

The plastic Automatic Binding Bricks looked great. They also worked better than the old wooden bricks had—at first. Very soon, though, it became clear that the new bricks had some problems. The first problem was the plastic itself. LEGO was using a material called **cellulose acetate** that did not hold its shape very well. The bricks tended to warp. Their colors also faded over time.

The way the bricks locked together was also a problem. The LEGO company calls this "clutch power." The bricks did lock together, but not as well as they wanted them

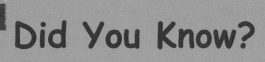

Did You Know?

Silly Putty was introduced at the International Toy Fair in New York in 1950, the year after Ole Kirk Christiansen began making his interlocking plastic bricks.

to. Some bricks were too tight. Others were too loose. If the bricks started to warp, the fit got even worse. Children became discouraged. Their Automatic Binding Bricks just did not work the way they were supposed to.

These problems hurt the company's sales. Packages of Automatic Binding Bricks sat on toy store shelves for months. After a while, some store owners sent the bricks back to LEGO and asked for their money back. It seemed that Ole Christiansen's idea might turn into a costly mistake.

How LEGO Bricks Work

Basic LEGO bricks have studs on top and tubes on the inside. The studs are slightly wider than the spaces between the tubes and the outer walls. When two bricks slide together, one brick's studs bend the other brick's walls and tubes slightly. The walls and tubes, however, want to keep their shape. They push against the studs as they try to return to their original position. This push creates enough pressure to hold the bricks together.

But the Christiansens were not ready to give up. They still thought that plastic toys were the future. The company kept making and selling its Automatic Binding Bricks, which were renamed LEGO Bricks (*LEGO Mursten* in Danish) in 1953.

A New Direction

By this time, Godtfred had become a leader in the LEGO **Group**. He helped with every part of the company's business, from design to sales. More and more, his ideas were shaping changes in LEGO toys.

One day Godtfred had a **brainstorm**. He realized that there were many toys for children, but no "system of play." A system of play would involve sets of toys. A child could build parts of a set or a whole set. Either way, children could mix and match the parts any way they wanted. Godtfred got right to work on his idea. By 1955 the LEGO company had 28 themed sets. One of the first themed sets was the "Town Plan." It included enough bricks to make a house, a gas station, or another building. The finished buildings could be grouped together to make LEGO towns. Kids then added LEGO cars, trees, and street signs to complete their projects.

As Godtfred had predicted, the LEGO System of Play was hugely popular. It was so popular, in fact, that the Christiansens decided it was time to expand their company. They started selling LEGO sets in Sweden. They also opened a sales office in Germany. Just as they had hoped, sales of LEGO toys shot up.

Getting It Right

But the old problems of fading colors, warping bricks, and a less-than-snug fit had never been solved. Godtfred decided it was time to deal with these problems.

A typical LEGO set like this one includes scenery, buildings, and people.

First up was clutch power. The bricks needed to fit together better. LEGO designers added plastic tubes to the undersides of the bricks. The tubes made the bricks sturdier and more stable. They also acted like extra walls, helping the bricks cling together more snugly. The redesigned bricks came out in 1958. They were a big improvement.

This **milestone** would be the last for Ole Kirk Christiansen. LEGO's founder died in March 1958. Godtfred took his father's place as the leader of the LEGO Group.

A Push for Excellence

Godtfred continued the push for excellence. He kept looking for ways to improve LEGO bricks. He felt sure he had found the answer in 1963, when a new plastic called **ABS (acrylonitrile butadiene styrene)** became available. This substance did not warp or lose its color, as the old cellulose acetate had. It had other pluses. It was not **toxic**. It did not rust. And it resisted heat, acids, salt, and oils. In

Drop, Squeeze, and Bite

To stick together properly, LEGO bricks must be exactly the right shape and size. LEGO employees therefore measure samples often during the production process. They also drop bricks, squeeze them, and even bite them to make sure they are sturdy. Only 18 out of every 1 million bricks fail the test.

short, it seemed to be the perfect toy-making material.

Godtfred decided that all LEGO toys would be made of the wonderful new plastic. Before long, ABS bricks were rolling off the company's manufacturing lines. These bricks were exactly the same as the ones sold today. They were sturdy and colorful. They fit together well. They were almost impossible to destroy. And, because of careful manufacturing, the bricks were exactly the same size from one set to another. This meant that all LEGO pieces fit together perfectly, no matter where or when they were bought or which set they came in.

LEGO bricks undergo testing to make sure they are heat resistant.

More Ideas

Many more new ideas followed. One involved engine power. Starting in 1966, kids could buy and build LEGO trains with real working motors. The trains chugged

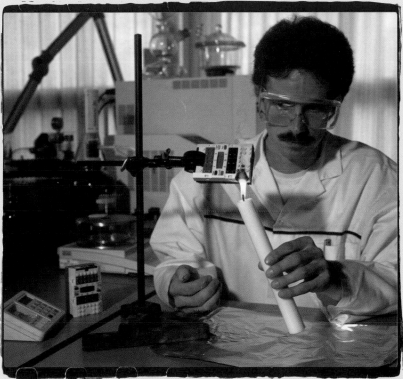

Godtfred introduced the idea of themed playsets, such as this garage, in the 1950s.

their way around electric rails that kids snapped together themselves. Still sold today, the trains and tracks have been redesigned several times. The modern designs, however, still work with the company's earliest train sets. The company calls this feature "backwards engineering." This means that designers consider old products when thinking about new ones. They want all LEGO pieces, no matter their age, to fit into the overall System of Play.

This idea was important in the development of another LEGO **product line**, called DUPLO. Launched in 1969, DUPLO bricks were exactly twice as big along every dimension—width, length, and height—as regular LEGO bricks. They were designed to snap easily onto standard-size bricks. Because they were larger, though, they were much easier for small children to use. Now young kids could enjoy the LEGO System of Play alongside their older brothers and sisters.

Minifigs Arrive

Another big change took place in 1974, when plastic people joined the LEGO world. The first people were part of a set called "LEGO Family." This kit included a mother, father, daughter, son, and

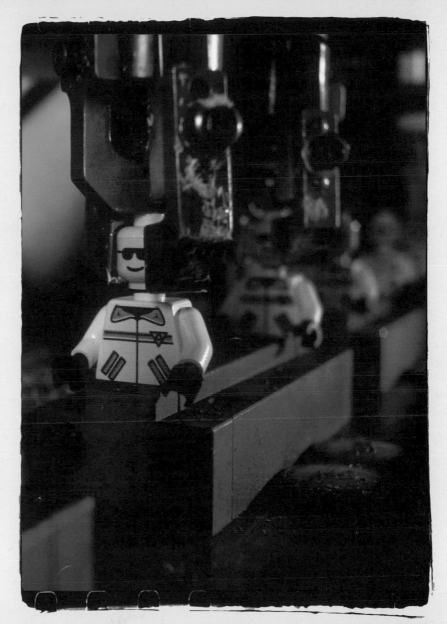

Minifigs come off the assembly line. Every playset has its own minifigs.

grandmother. The figures were too big to work with other LEGO sets. Still, they were an instant hit with both boys and girls. Seeing this, LEGO developed a group of smaller people that could snap onto regular LEGO bricks.

The new people were called miniature figures, or minifigs for short. They had movable arms and legs and smiling yellow faces. Since 1974, more than 4 billion LEGO minifigs have been produced. They now come with many mix-and-match parts. These include hair, hats, helmets, tools, eyeglasses, goggles, shields, swords, capes, armor, and more.

The Joy of Building

As the years went by, more and more LEGO toys were added. The company introduced sets with themes such as outer space, pirates, dinosaurs, airports, the Wild West, and many more. The company also came out with more complex kits for advanced builders and started to base some sets on movies and television shows. The first movie-themed set, "LEGO Star Wars," appeared in 1999. By 2007, the list included Winnie the Pooh, Jurassic Park, Harry Potter, Batman, Spider-Man, and SpongeBob SquarePants.

LEGO sets include minifigs that kids can use in the LEGO structure they build.

The Town Plan Returns

In January 2008 the LEGO Group brought back one of its original sets, the "Town Plan." This set marked the company's 50th anniversary. The new set has 1,981 pieces. It includes a 1950s-style gas station with pumps, a car wash and garage, a town hall with a newly married couple, a movie theater and ticket booth, seats and posters, two cars, and eight minifigs.

With all of the changes to the LEGO toy line over the years, one thing has not changed. For lots of kids, the joy of building with LEGO toys is coming up with their own designs. Nathaniel Macmillan of Novato, California, is one of those kids. In 2005, 14-year-old Nathaniel was named champion in the "LEGO Brick to the Future: 2055" Building Challenge. Nathaniel's entry, "Town 100 Community Center," earned him the title of champion along with a $5,000 grand prize scholarship. Nathaniel has been building with LEGO toys since he was 2 years old. What keeps him coming back? "What I like about building with LEGO bricks," Nathaniel says, "is that you can express your creativity and it's something you can touch, not just do on paper."

Chapter 3

A World of Change

At the Massachusetts Institute of Technology (MIT), students build and race LEGO cars. It feels like playtime. But there is something else going on here. These students are in the middle of a lesson. They are learning about **mechanical engineering** and design. In another room, other students use LEGO bricks to show how cells divide. These students are learning about cells and DNA, one of the building blocks of life.

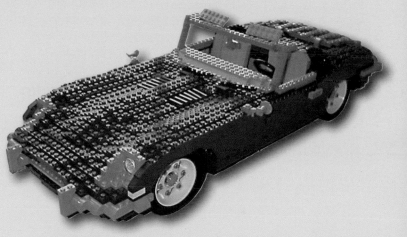

By building elaborate LEGO cars like this one, students can learn about engineering and design.

These two lessons are part of a program run by the Edgerton Center at MIT. MIT is well known for its work in science and technology. The program is aimed at getting young students excited about science.

Other schools have found different ways of teaching with LEGO bricks. They are used in classrooms at all age levels, from preschool to college. They are used for teaching math, science, language skills, and engineering.

Making a Movie

They are also used in other ways. Lewis Roberts, 12, is making a movie. In his movie, raptors chase LEGO **castaways** trying to flee on a LEGO raft. Lewis is one of eight boys taking part in a special program for young people with autism. Autism is a disorder that affects the brain. Among other things, it affects how a person communicates and **interacts** with others.

Toying with Technology

Students at Iowa State University design and build simple models of an elevator and its controller, a garage door and its opener, a computer-controlled car, and a house security system. And they do all of this with LEGO kits and small microcomputers. They are taking part in a class for students studying to be teachers. The goal is to give them a simple introduction to electronics. The class is called "Toying with Technology." It was started by a professor in the late 1990s. It continues to be a popular course, both at the university and with K-12 students and teachers.

At a clinic in Voorhees, Pennsylvania, Lewis and the other boys are learning social skills. They are learning to talk, plan, and work together. And their LEGO characters are at the center of all of this activity. During the session, the boys take on different roles. They act as engineers, builders, and suppliers. In these roles, they must talk to each other and work together. The engineer's design has to be acceptable to the builder. And the builder has to get parts from the supplier.

Lewis's mother, Karen Roberts, says the LEGO sessions are helping him learn to get along with others. "I feel bringing Lewis here has brought him out of himself," she says. "He's loved LEGO since he was a tiny kid."

Working in a group to build LEGO sets such as this one of Essex House can teach students how to cooperate and direct projects.

Problem Solving

LEGO toys have found other uses too. Some companies have turned to LEGO toys to improve themselves. Under a program called LEGO Serious Play, companies divide workers into teams. The teams are given building challenges. They are asked to work together to solve those challenges. The goal is to improve teamwork and problem solving skills among workers.

One company that did this is eBay, the online auction Web site. A spokesman for eBay said it was a good team-building exercise. "It left us an even stronger and more **agile** team," he said.

The LEGO Impact

LEGO sets are sold in more than 130 countries around the world. To keep up with its fans, the company now has offices in the United States, the United Kingdom, Australia, Japan, China, Russia, Mexico, and many other nations.

Playing and building are still the most popular things to do with LEGO products. Every day, children around the world prove

Nathan Sawaya, LEGO Whiz

Nathan Sawaya is known around the world for his amazing LEGO sculptures. His creations include a model of the Brooklyn Bridge, a full-size tyrannosaurus rex, and a 10-foot (3m) speedboat. Once a LEGO employee, Sawaya now has his own LEGO art studio in New York. His work appears in museums all over the United States. In 2007 it was featured in a solo show called "The Art of the Brick" at the Museum of Art in Lancaster, New York.

A former LEGO employee, Nathan Sawaya now creates pieces of art using LEGO bricks.

that the Christiansens were **visionaries**. With LEGO bricks, they gave the world a new way to play.

Systems of Play

LEGO's success did not just affect children. It affected other toymakers as well. In the mid-1960s, other companies noticed how well LEGO products were selling. Many of these companies came out with their own "systems of play" in response. A doll, for instance, might not be the only item purchased. Now, there might be a whole line of clothes that kids could buy in addition. Or a basic train set could be expanded later with add-on tracks, cars, and buildings.

This idea has become very important in the toy industry. The most popular toys today are actually groups or lines of toys, not one-of-a-kind items. By following the LEGO example, companies around the globe have won new fans and boosted their sales.

Fans for Life

LEGO users are very loyal. They do not just play with LEGO toys, they want to talk about them and share their favorite models as well. To help this happen, the company has created a special club for preteens. The LEGO Club lets its 2.4 million members swap design photos online. It also sends out a newsletter every other month. The newsletter tells members about the latest LEGO events and products.

LEGO Club membership ends when a child reaches the age of thirteen. Many people, though, refuse to give up LEGO toys as they grow. These people often stay

LEGO was the first company to come out with themed play sets, such as this garage play set that includes cars and minifigs with the gas station.

LEGO enthusiasts of all ages have fun at LEGOLAND and view remarkable things made entirely of LEGOs.

connected by joining all-ages LEGO clubs. These clubs have no official connection with the LEGO Group. They are run by their members, who call themselves Adult Fans of LEGO (AFOLs). The clubs usually have their own Web sites and events. They may also help to set up national or international LEGO conventions. The biggest convention, LEGO World, takes place in the Netherlands. This annual event attracts up to 60,000 visitors.

Most AFOLs just want to play. But some take their interest a step further. They share their knowledge as LEGO ambassadors. Ambassadors are official but nonpaid representatives of the LEGO Group. To earn this position, they must be very good at LEGO construction. They must also be enthusiastic and professional.

LEGOLAND

LEGOLAND theme parks show just how much fun LEGO toys can be. In these parks, millions of bricks have been used to create amazing LEGO models and attractions. The parks also feature rides and hands-on play areas. The largest park, LEGOLAND Billund (Denmark), opened in 1968. It attracts 1.6 million visitors each year. Other parks include LEGOLAND Windsor (England); LEGOLAND Deutschland (Gunzburg, Germany); and LEGOLAND California (Carlsbad, California). The newest LEGOLAND is slated to open in 2011 in the Middle East in Dubai.

Some LEGO ambassadors visit schools or conventions. Others are active online or through local clubs. Whichever method they choose, all ambassadors agree to share their skills and knowledge with other LEGO users.

Chapter 4

The Cutting Edge

In April 2007, a team of seventh-graders from Portland, Oregon, won an international contest for LEGO robot builders. The team, named Pigmice, competed against 94 teams from 22 countries. Their robot performed certain tasks better than all the others. And their presentation to the judges was equally good. They came away with the championship at the Nano Quest World Festival in Atlanta, Georgia.

Speaking before the Atlanta event, one team member described why she gets so much enjoyment out of building with LEGO robots. "LEGO robots changed me," says Olivia Bolles. "I'm convinced. It combines art, engineering, math, science, writing, teamwork, friends, and fun into something I love."

This event and others like it show just how much toys have changed in recent decades. Technology has given kids many

A group of experienced builders put these MINDSTORMS robots together at the Microsoft campus in Redmond, Washington.

new ways to play. Electronics, computers, and video-based toys are especially big hits. Children who love these things are not always interested in old-fashioned LEGO bricks.

To satisfy lovers of technology, the LEGO Group now has toys that combine the old and new. These products are bringing LEGO toys to a whole new group of children.

LEGO MINDSTORMS

The most technical LEGO product line is called MINDSTORMS. The first MIND-STORMS sets were introduced in 1998. They included motors, touch sensors, and light sensors. These items snapped together with regular LEGO bricks and other special parts. Kids could use MIND-STORMS pieces to build their own robots. They could then write software programs to control the robots. The programs were stored in computerized LEGO bricks that acted as the robots' "brains."

Did You Know?

The LEGO Group got some high-level help in developing MINDSTORMS. The MIND-STORMS kits were developed through a partnership with the Massachusetts Institute of Technology (MIT). MIT is well known for its work in science and technology.

A worker assembles LEGO MINDSTORMS programmable bricks. The bricks can control LEGO robots.

A robotic LEGO vehicle rolls through a maze erected at an Italian museum.

The first MINDSTORMS kits were very successful. The company then updated MINDSTORMS in 2006 to MINDSTORMS NXT. NXT kits include a brick- shaped computer that can control four sensors and three motors. The computer also has a video screen and a speaker. It can be programmed via computer and controlled by a user's cell phone. This is the type of LEGO robot the Pigmice of Oregon used in their winning entry.

Sharing Ideas

Many MINDSTORMS users enjoy sharing their programs and ideas online. The LEGO Group encourages these conversations. It hosts a Web chat site where users can get

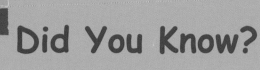

Did You Know?

In 2000, the LEGO toy line was named "Toy of the Century" by *Fortune* magazine and by the British Toy Retailers Association.

together. The LEGO Group also organizes an annual competition, FIRST LEGO League, where young MINDSTORMS users can meet each other in real life. At this competition, prizes are given to the best MINDSTORMS robots. Held in the Netherlands, the 2007 event attracted more than 100,000 competitors from around the globe.

LEGO Digital Designer

MINDSTORMS has a strong following. Many LEGO fans, however, prefer basic plastic bricks. They enjoy using these bricks to build original LEGO art. Depending on the skill of the user, these creations can be very simple or very complex. The bigger the sculpture, the more time, talent, and bricks it takes.

There is no way to cut corners when developing a design idea. But there are software programs that can help. LEGO Group has a software program called LEGO Digital Designer. It has become a handy tool for LEGO lovers everywhere.

The idea behind Digital Designer is simple. The program is downloaded free of charge from the LEGO Web site. A person uses the program to create a **virtual** LEGO model. The model is then sent back to the LEGO Web site. LEGO computers "read" the image and figure out which bricks are needed to build it. The user simply clicks the "buy" button to order those bricks. A few days later, the custom package arrives at the designer's home.

LEGO Digital Designer is unique in that it combines classic LEGO play with cutting-edge technology. With nearly 800 styles of bricks, it also provides almost limitless possibilities for creating new models and scenes. It allows users to "play well" in ways LEGO's founders never could have imagined.

Professor Kevin Warwick (left) plays with robots with a research student. These robots have been built using LEGO MINDSTORMS kits.

LEGO Media

Creating designs is not the only way to enjoy LEGO toys on the computer. Many games also bring LEGO bricks and characters into the digital world. One is "LEGO Rock Raiders." In that game, players help computerized minifigs to drill and dig their way through rocky caves. In "LEGO Chess," minifigs become living pawns on an animated chessboard. Other popular games include "LEGO Star Wars," "LEGO Batman," and "LEGO Indiana Jones."

For users who prefer to go online, short LEGO films can provide entertainment. These films are usually called "LEGO movies" or "brickfilms." Most of them are made by fans. They feature moving, talking minifigs and other LEGO products.

They are created with a technique called stop-motion animation. In this process, the filmmaker takes thousands of pictures. Each picture is a tiny bit different from the one before it. When the pictures are viewed one after another, very quickly, the illusion of motion is created. LEGO toys have also appeared in comics, puzzle books, cartoons, music videos, and many other types of media. There are also LEGO watches, pens, backpacks, T-shirts, coats, lunch boxes, and much more. Today, there are endless ways for LEGO fans to show their loyalty.

Nothing Matches the Original

This loyalty has not stopped other companies from trying to copy the success of LEGO. One Canadian company sells a line

A full-size LEGO Indiana Jones is displayed at the Toy Fair in New York in 2008.

Chief Engineer Per Knudsen looks up at the LEGO tower located in the United Kingdom, which is thought to have broken the world record for the tallest tower made from LEGO bricks. The structure is thought to contain nearly 500,000 LEGO bricks and stands at nearly 100 feet high.

LEGO products, they come in different sizes for different age groups. Brightly colored and inexpensive, these bricks are found in toy stores all over North America.

A Chinese company also sells LEGO-like products. These bricks and minifigs work the same way LEGO toys do. They can even snap together with LEGO products. However, they do not cost as much, which is part of their appeal. Competition from other companies has made things harder for the LEGO Group. It has not, however, changed the way people feel about genuine LEGO products. In a way, it is even a compliment. It proves that Ole Kirk Christiansen's vision has stood the test of time. After more than 50 years, LEGO bricks are still a great idea.

of building bricks called MEGA Bloks. Like LEGO bricks, MEGA Bloks have studded tops and snap together. Also like

ABS (acrylonitrile butadiene styrene): A plastic commonly used to make toys, musical instruments, plumbing, and many other objects. Since 1963, all LEGO bricks have been made of ABS.

agile: Able to change or move easily.

brainstorm: A sudden, bright idea.

castaways: People who are shipwrecked.

cautious: Moving slowly and avoiding quick decisions.

cellulose acetate: The plastic used to make the earliest LEGO bricks.

child psychologist: A person who works with children and is an expert in the study of the mind and how it works.

designs: Plans for how something should be made.

durability: The ability to resist wear and tear.

flaws: Marks or faults that cause something to not be perfect.

Group: A collection of businesses under the direction of one main business.

hygienic: To be clean.

interacts: To have an effect on each other.

interlocking: Fitting into each other.

master carpenter: A skilled woodworker.

mechanical engineering: A branch of science that deals with the design and development of machines.

milestone: An important event or stage in life or history.

motto: A phrase that expresses the aims of a company.

patented: Protected by law against competition for a fixed period of time.

plastic: A manmade substance that can be given any permanent shape by molding under pressure and high heat.

polystyrene: A kind of hard plastic.

product line: A group of related items made by a particular company.

toxic: Poisonous.

virtual: Existing only in the computer world.

visionaries: People who make clear, strong, and usually correct predictions about the future.

Book

David Pickering, Nick Turpin, and Caryn Jenner, eds., The Ultimate LEGO Book. New York: DK, 1999.

Web Sites to Visit

Brickfilms (www.brickfilms.com). Amateur animators from all over the world post LEGO movies on this site.

FIRST LEGO League (www.firstlego league.org). At this site, visitors can get information and applications for upcoming MINDSTORMS NXT competitions.

LEGO (www.lego.com). The official LEGO Web site includes free games, message boards, clubs, and a virtual LEGO store.

LEGO Digital Designer (ldd.lego.com). Download a free copy of LEGO's Digital Designer software from this site.

LEGOLAND (www.legoland.com). Read about all four LEGOLAND theme parks on this fun, interactive site.

Nathan Sawaya: The Art of the Brick (www.brickartist.com). The world's most famous LEGO artist has posted pictures of his best creations on his personal Web site.

Index

About the Author

Kris Hirschmann has written nearly 200 books for children. Hirschmann lives just outside Orlando, Florida, with her husband, Michael, and her daughters, Nikki and Erika.